ARTS AND CRAFTS
DISCOVERY UNITS

- Let's Discover WEAVING

  Let's Discover Puppets

  Let's Discover Paper

  Let's Discover Watercolor

  Let's Discover Mobiles

  Let's Discover Tempera

  Let's Discover Papier-Mache

  Let's Discover Printing

  Let's Discover Crayon

  Let's Discover Tissue

LET'S DISCOVER WEAVING

Jenean Romberg

Arts and Crafts Discovery Units

The Center for Applied Research in Education, Inc.
521 Fifth Avenue, New York, N.Y. 10017

© 1975

THE CENTER FOR APPLIED
RESEARCH IN EDUCATION, INC.
NEW YORK

ACKNOWLEDGMENTS

*With love and thanks to my sister,
Sandy Kincaid, and my aunt, Marie V.
Howes, for their "unending patient
help" in preparing these manuscripts.*

Library of Congress Cataloging in Publication Data

Romberg, Jenean.
    Let's discover weaving.

    (Her Arts and crafts discovery units)
    1. Hand weaving—Study and teaching (Elementary)
2. Creative activities and seat work. I. Title.
TT848.R63   746.1'4   75-16263
ISBN 0-87628-532-9

PRINTED IN THE UNITED STATES OF AMERICA

Let's Discover . . .

Crayons . . . paper . . . paint . . . paste . . . scissors . . . the list of materials available for creative activities is endless. But it makes little difference how many exciting materials are available if we do not know how to use them and do not realize their potential. It is important to take the time to explore the uses and limitations of different media, materials, and techniques, become skillful in their uses, and learn what we, personally, can or cannot do.

The LET'S DISCOVER . . . series provides a broad exploration of basic materials, utilizing a wide variety of tools and techniques as well as manipulative and organizational skills. Each of its ten parts includes dozens of activities selected to meet special moods and occasions, and it is sequentially organized to allow a progression from very simple techniques in one media, to more complex techniques involving several media. The techniques are designed to enable anyone to achieve fascinating and intriguing effects so that those important "initial" experiences with a particular medium are positive and rewarding.

It is natural for each of us to want to make things, to experiment and explore. After gaining confidence and knowledge we then feel secure enough to be inventive, to express individual ideas, take pride and gain satisfaction in creativity. By choosing and creating colors, textures, and shapes, we share something of ourselves with others.

Let's explore, experiment, create!

Jenean Romberg

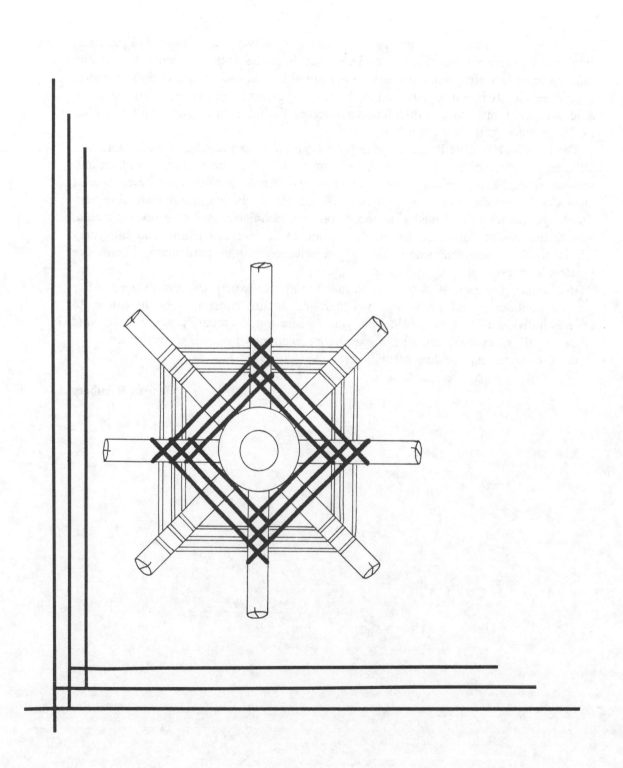

contents . . .

about weaving

Weaving is the process of crossing and interlacing threads at right angles to each other. As an art form it is much more than this. It is a means of creative expression, stimulating the designer-weaver to make discriminatory decisions in the use of color, texture, and shape; to fuse ideas, materials, and function into an aesthetic whole. An ancient art, weaving was first done with grasses woven with the fingers. Inevitably, new materials led to more sophisticated techniques and designs, alive with color and rich in texture.

The activities in this unit present weaving with a minimum of technical terminology. They offer the inexperienced as well as the experienced weaver a variety of experiences in weaving without a conventional loom. Emphasis is placed on the simplicity of the weaving device and the availability of materials used. Very few special tools are needed to construct the so-called looms utilized here, but work with even the simplest device provides a challenge and satisfying creative results. The principles of weaving are introduced with the use of paper. The basic techniques involved in cutting and weaving warp and weft familiarize the beginner with the weaving process. All, it is hoped, will help the weaver in developing a creative approach with methods and materials and a personal approach to weaving.

WELCOME TO THE WORLD OF WEAVING!

techniques with weaving

Weaving is the process of crossing and interlacing threads at right angles to each other.

warp: the vertical threads (strings) which make up the "skeleton" across which the weft threads are woven to form cloth or web.

weft: the horizontal threads woven across the warp to form cloth.

shot: one length of weft thread across the warp.
selvage: edge threads of the warp.
tension: the degree of tightness at which the warp is stretched.

three basic weaves

All weaving patterns are derived from the three basic weaves. By combining parts of the basic weaves or by combining two entirely basic weaves, completely new patterns are created.

plain or 'tabby' weave:

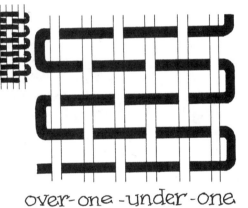

over-one-under-one

is the most common, consisting of over-one-under-one. The weft thread is crossed over one warp thread, under the next, over the next, etc. On the return shot this is reversed: under-one-over-one, so the next weft thread goes under the warp and so forth.

Variations of the tabby weave:

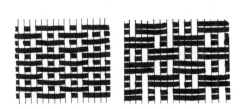

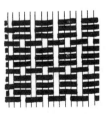

basket weave: consists of going under-two-over-two or under-three-over-three.

These consist of two or three rows of over-one-under-one and then two or three rows of under-one-over-one.

HINT: Since the weft thread must always go around the selvage thread but sometimes cannot go over or under according to the pattern count, it may be necessary to change the count, going over or under the selvage thread in order to get the next shot correct. All adjustments are made on the selvage.

twill weave:

consists of over-two-under-two, each successive shot (row) the same, *but* moving over one warp thread, so that of any pair of warp threads crossed over in one shot, only one of that pair is crossed over in the next shot. This weave produces diagonal lines on the surface of the cloth. It will be a right-hand or a left-hand twill, depending on the direction the diagonal lines take.

Adjustments may have to be made to make the pattern work out at the selvage edges.

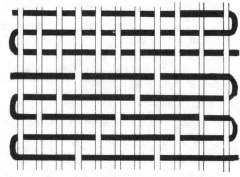

right-hand twill

left-hand twill

over-two-under-two

satin weave:

consists of over-three-under-one or over-one-under-three. This weave is generally used when desiring to bring either the warp or the weft to the surface without having a set pattern to the weave. When going over-three-under-one, the weave is tight and the warp will not show. By reversing the weave—over-one-under-three—the warp will dominate the design. Adjustments will have to be made at the selvage edges to make the pattern work.

under-three-over-one

over-three-under-one

other techniques:

weaver's knot:

used to attach the end of the weft thread to the warp thread when beginning to weave.

weaver's knot using double weft threads.

piecing the yarn:

to add new weft threads during the weaving, lay the new thread beside the old one, weaving in exactly the same pattern, overlapping for about 1½″, and then beat into place with a beater. This eliminates unsightly knots. Ends can be tucked into weft when the weaving is completed.

tapestry slit

weaving partway across the warp and back again, leaving an open area in the pattern. This device was used in olden days to change from one color to another, and then the slits were sewn up when the tapestry came off the loom. Slits can be used to add decorative effects but should be planned so they don't look like a series of mistakes or holes.

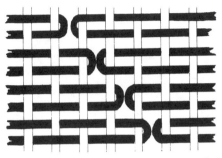

diagonal tapestry slit

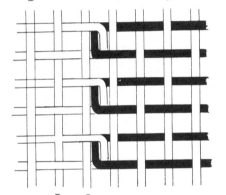

staggered tapestry slit

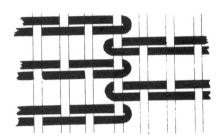

dovetailing

two or more rows of weft are woven alternately around a common warp. Two colors meeting make a decorative serrated pattern.

interlocking

the basic technique of linking areas of adjacent weft threads, similar or different in color; locks shapes to the background. Weave the shapes first and then weave up to their sides with the background color, weaving each lock as it is reached.

chain stitch

helps to space the warps evenly and holds them into place. This stitch can also be used to outline shapes.

Egyptian knot:

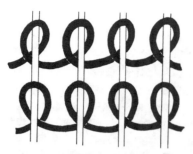

the weft loops around the warp, creating a knot-like weave. The needle goes under two warps, back over one; every wrap looks like a bead of yarn. Turning around is difficult. Wrap the outside warp twice and then under and around the next warp, then continue as before.

soumak loops:

an Oriental stitch or knot: over two warps and back under one or forward four loops and back under two. Alternate with a row of plain weave so the loops go in the same direction; the plain weave also gives strength and durability.

Ghiordes knot:

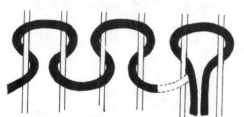

adds lots of texture. Loops may be cut or left continuous; the fuzzy ends provide more texture than loops. To gauge size of loops an object such as a pencil may be inserted while making.

fringe:

cut pieces of yarn, twice as long as fringe desired; fold in half and attach to edge of weaving or warp loops as illustrated:

tassels:

wind yarn around cardboard cut to size tassel desired, winding it twenty or more times around, depending upon the thickness of yarn and plumpness of tassel required. Tie strands tightly together around top; clip other end of strands. Wrap a piece of yarn tightly around strands a few times; tie and knot.

techniques with looms:

The following looms are used for the activities in this book. Very few tools are needed to construct these looms. Emphasis has been placed on the simplicity of the weaving device and the availability of the materials used. Since most weaving techniques can be incorporated in almost all of the activities, there will a reference only to the particular kind of loom to be used for each activity.

paper:

cardboard:

burlap:

cotton mesh:

scrim:

wire:

a wooden loom:

a spool:

with straws:

ojo de dios:

a hanger:

branch

a branch:

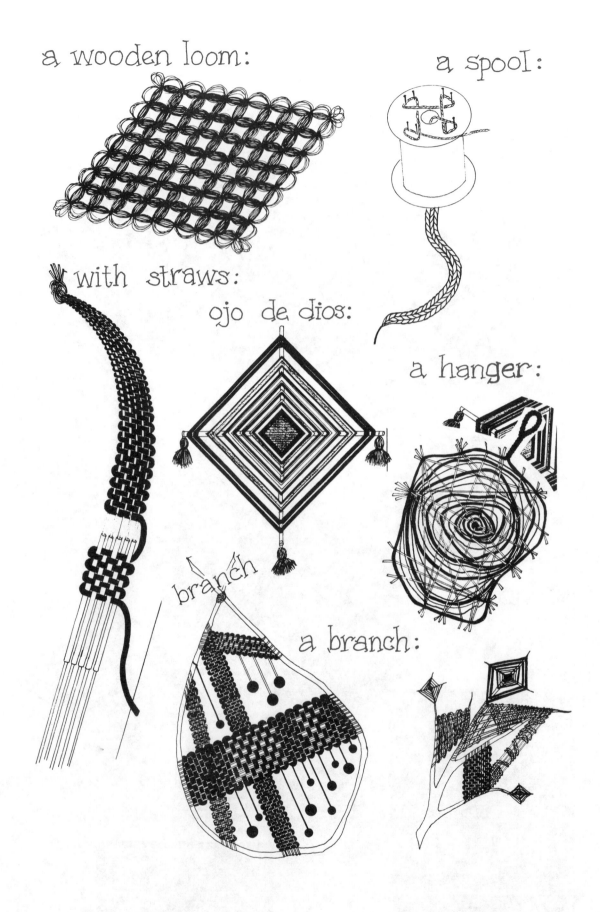

14

preparing for weaving

format

—each activity begins with a list of materials needed for each individual.

—all supplies listed are generally those available in the schools, or easy to find and inexpensive.

—directions are simple and to the point, with illustrations to demonstrate each step while still allowing for the greatest freedom of individual expression.

—illustrations and directions for those methods and techniques common to all activities are given in the front of the book and referred to when needed.

—if there is a question about the materials needed, refer to the "Materials" section at the front of the book for further explanation.

—at the end of each activity there are suggestions for variations of the project, or perhaps a suggestion for making things go well.

—almost all of the projects, with a little adaptation or simplification, can be used with any age level.

—the illustrations and captions for each activity are simply for suggestion. Show samples, demonstrate and give examples, but then let the students go from there, and they will—beautifully!

—the activities and their variations do not necessarily need to be taught in sequence, but many times an introduction to a media through the use of beginning simple activities will provide more confidence for tackling more complicated activities.

materials

The following materials are needed to do the activities in this book:

for looms:

· cardboard: stiff carton type, chipboard, heavier type gift boxes, illustration board, shoe box lids, cardboard containers: cottage cheese, oats, powdered soap, sour cream

· wooden: 1″ x 1″ soft pine, length and width desired; old picture frames, stretcher frames, wooden boxes

· miscellaneous: wooden spools, straws, twigs, branches, hangers, dowel rods, wire

weaving into -

wire mesh—comes in a variety of types; the gauge determines the size of the hole and the weight or thickness of the wire

wire mesh　　　　　　window screen　　　　　　chicken wire

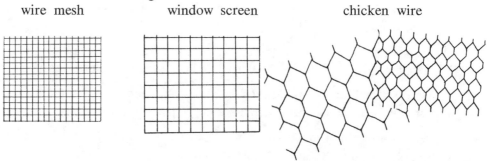

cotton mesh—available in curtains, mosquito netting, onion bags and dish cloths. It may also be purchased by the yard or collected from scraps.

scrim—sometimes called cross-stitch rug canvas; fairly large holes permit thread or yarn to be easily pushed or pulled through; can be purchased or scraps collected (try hobby shops, needlework shops for free scraps).

· paper: all kinds; complete list on page 19.

the warp:

The warp must be strong enough to withstand the weaving process, but does not necessarily need to be made of thick or heavy yarns. Some synthetic yarns are almost gossamer fine and yet are extremely strong.

Recommended:　wrapping twine　　heavy string　　kite string　　jute
　　　　　　　　cotton warp　　　linen cord　　heavy yarn

the weft:

Weaving is a craft of touching as well as seeing. The way a yarn feels between the fingers will guide and inspire—as well as limit—the way it can be used. Before beginning to weave, make a collection of the following:

· found, collected, purchased:
cotton roving; variety of yarns (wool, synthetic, cotton, metallic, rayon, crewel, rug, tapestry); jute; mohair; unraveled old sweaters; novelty yarns.

Wrap yarn in loose balls. To store easily place in a covered container such as a coffee can or cottage cheese carton. Punch a hole in the lid and pull the end of the yarn through the hole. This keeps the yarns from becomming tangled and knotted.

- "bits and pieces":

ribbon	fabric scraps	felt strips	reeds
buttons	rickrack	velvet	beads
raffia	hem tape scraps	bells	lace
leather strips	pipe cleaners		

- native materials:

twigs	pine needles	stems	cornhusks
grasses	cattails	leaves	vines
barley	seedpots	wheat	shells

tools:

- shuttle: an instrument used for passing the weft thread from one edge of the cloth (loom) to the other between the threads of the warp. A shuttle can be made using one of the following methods:

an ice cream stick
or tongue depressor

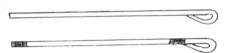

piece of heavy wire bent and bound with cloth tape

—for weaving in tight places or small items, a large-eyed needle such as those used for needlepoint or crewel embroidery works the best.

- beater: used to push woven weft threads into place so the weave is uniform and consistent. A wide-toothed comb of any kind works well.

other materials:

wire cutters	T-pins	newsprint
finishing nails	straight pins	crayons
common nails	paste	felt tip pens
hammer	white glue	staples
ruler	stapler	
pencil	paper punch	

mounting:

dowel or wooden rod	thin strips of wood	reeds	wire

The finished weaving may be left on the loom or transferred. To remove, carefully lift the warp loops from the nails or notches at one end of the loom and push a dowel rod through the series of loops. Then remove the warp at the other end and place a dowel through those loops. The weight of the dowels causes the finished piece to hang straight. If more weight is needed, small metal weights can be attached to the back of the weaving, or interesting objects such as bells, beads, clay pieces, etc., as well as fringe may be added to the bottom of the weaving, both to be decorative and to add the weight needed to hang properly.

getting ready – go!

—always have the materials ready!

—try the activity yourself before presenting it; you will be more aware of the techniques and knowledge needed as well as the pitfalls to be avoided.

—do demonstrate. Your free use of materials and your approach will encourage others; care, use of materials and basic skills can be demonstrated at the same time.

—don't be afraid to have a demonstration turn out a failure; if it does, discuss why.

—allow plenty of time in which to complete each project; divide into two or more working sessions if necessary.

—encourage individuality and originality; remind students not to be "cameras."

—encourage the student to discover things for himself, to be resourceful.

—allow the students to experiment and make mistakes.

—do let the students share their work with each other while they are working or when the activity is completed. It's exciting—and often motivating—to see what others are doing.

—display the work of all students; encourage students to exhibit their work so that everyone can enjoy it.

—MOST OF ALL, MAKE ART A HAPPY HAPPENING!

weaving with paper

The principles of weaving are easily introduced with the use of paper. The basic techniques involved in cutting and weaving warp and weft familiarize the beginner with the weaving process. Experience will lead to the discovery of ways to vary the warp and weft, as well as the manner in which the strips are woven, to create more intricate and aesthetic designs.

MATERIALS:

paper—types of paper which may be used for weaving include:

construction	crepe	cellophane
tissue	blotting	glazed
gift wrap	shelf	wallpaper
colorful tagboard	pages from	newspaper
metallic	magazines	

· Collect papers for a period of time before initiating weaving projects. Look for colorful and textured papers to stimulate the imagination and inspire ideas. Interesting weaving patterns can be made by using assorted papers or by combining rough and smooth, shiny and dull papers, or by using various color combinations.

· Use a heavier weight paper such as construction paper for the warp (base) for easier manipulation.

"bits and pieces"—other collected materials which may be combined with paper weaving include:

yarn	ribbon	string
raffia	shoestrings	rickrack
weeds	cloth	felt
twine	lace	straw

also needed—

scissors   ruler   pencil   glue or paste

optional—crayons, tempera and/or watercolor paints

DISCOVERY STEPS:

1. *Cutting the warp* (vertical strips):
   —Fold the piece of paper (any size desired) in half, horizontally. Place the folded paper on the work surface so the open edges are at the top. Draw a pencil line one inch down from the open edges, across the width of the paper.

—Cut strips of equal width, beginning at the fold line and cutting up to the pencil line near the open edges.

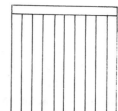

These lines may be measured and marked with pencil if absolute accuracy is desired.

—When cutting is complete, open and lay flat.

2. *Cutting the weft* (horizontal strips):

—The weft consists of strips of paper cut to various widths or all the same width. The most efficient and fastest way to cut a great number at one time is to use a paper cutter. Try ½″, ¼″, ¾″, 1″ and 1½″ strips of all kinds of paper.

—An alternative method for cutting a number of strips of equal width is to fold a 9″ x 12″ paper like a fan and then cut into strips, using the fold lines as a guide.

3. *Weaving the weft:*

—Begin with the traditional pattern, over-one-under-one, also referred to as the "tabby weave."

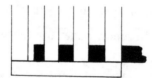

(a) Push the end of one strip under the first vertical strip and then over the second vertical strip. Continue across the width of the paper. When complete, push the strip as close as possible to the bottom of the paper.

(b) Begin the second strip by going over the first vertical strip and under the second. Continue, over and under, across the width of the paper.

(c) Continue in the same manner, repeating steps a and b, remembering to alternate the strips so that one strip goes over the warp while the next goes under the warp.

(d) Using glue or paste, secure ends of weft strips to sides of warp paper. Trim away ends. The illustration shows a paper weaving completed, using only the tabby weave.

variations:

The possibilities for exploration in paper weaving are endless. By changing the cut of the weft or the warp, entirely new patterns and designs are created. The following are but a few of the possibilities:

change the warp:

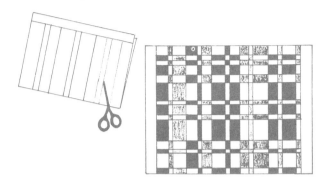

—vary the width of spaces between each cut of the warp and the width of the strips used for the weft.

—Cut warp and weft strips in very thin strips. Compare the results with "op art" paintings.

—Cut the warp to form irregular shapes. Weave straight strips through the warp.

—Completed examples:

—Extra-large shapes are created by weaving widely spaced, curved warp with wide straight weft strips.

—Try using the paper without folding; make a pencil line one inch from one edge. Cut warp strips, beginning at the opposite edge. The paper may be used vertically or horizontally.

—vertical:

—horizontal:

—Completed examples:

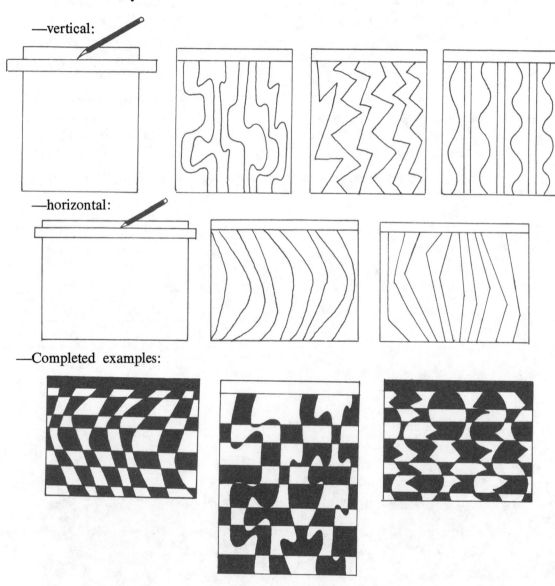

change the weft:

—Cut the warp in straight strips. Cut the weft strips to form irregular shapes:

—along one edge.

—along both edges.

—Paste or glue a narrow strip of contrasting color on the weft strip before weaving.

—Add polk-a-dots, other cut shapes made of printed papers or yarn to the weft strips before weaving.

—Weave weft under and over in different combinations: under one, over three and so forth. Refer to pages 9–12 for various weaving patterns.

—Paste or glue paper-sculptured shapes on top of squares formed by weaving, after it is completed.

—Use crayon, string, yarn or paint to accent certain areas.

—Using any of the techniques suggested in *Let's Discover Printing,* print on top surface of completed weaving.

using 'woven' paper:

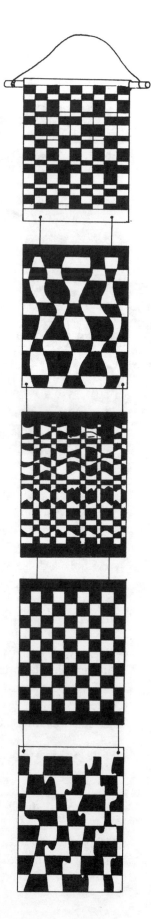

for folders:

a basket:

cover boxes and tins:

hanging panels:

jigsaw weaving

Technique: irregular warp and weft

MATERIALS:

1. two sheets of construction paper,
   9″ x 12″ or 12″ x 18″, different colors
2. scissors
3. ruler and pencil
4. paste or glue

DISCOVERY STEPS:

1. Draw a pencil line one inch down from the
   top, across the width of the paper. Cut
   gently curved lines, beginning at the bottom of
   the paper and cutting up to the pencil line. The
   curved pencil lines may be drawn with a pencil before
   cutting.

 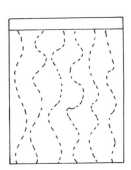

2. Cut curved strips across the width of the second sheet of paper, *one at a time*.
   Weave the cut strip into the other sheet of paper *right after it is cut*. Be sure to do
   this to avoid frustration and confusion, as each strip fits right next to the one pre-
   viously cut.

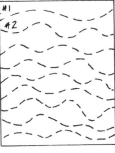 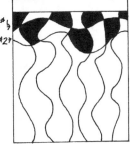

3. When weaving is completed, glue or paste all the ends down and trim the edges.

HINTS:

—Try using printed papers in combination with plain or printed papers or sheets
   from magazines.

...in simple shapes

Technique: paper weaving

MATERIALS:

1. (1) 9″ x 12″ medium-weight paper for shape
2. strips of paper for weft: varying in width and color
3. pencil and ruler
4. scissors
5. paste or glue

DISCOVERY STEPS:

1. Fold the paper in half, vertically or horizontally:

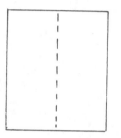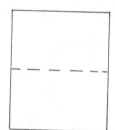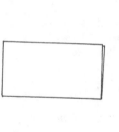

2. Draw a simple, symmetrical shape, center on the fold. (Refer to cutting symmetrical shapes in *Let's Discover Paper,* page 26.) Pencil in a margin approximately ½″ in from the open edges.

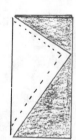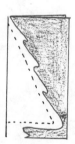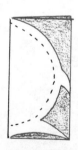

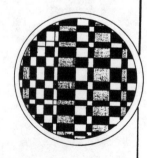

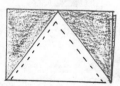

3. Cut out. Shaded areas in illustration above are those cut away.

4. Cut the weft strips, beginning at the fold and cutting to the pencil line. These can be straight, curved or zig-zag.

5. Weave in weft strips, using any colors or patterns desired. "Bits and pieces" may also be added for interest and variation.

6. When weaving is completed, paste or glue down ends. Trim excess paper from strips along edges of shapes. Any details may be added with crayons, paper, etc.

paper, bits n' pieces

Technique: paper weaving

MATERIALS:

1. (1) 9″ x 12″ or 12″ x 18″ construction paper any color
2. "bits and pieces": yarn, ribbon, rick-rack, metallic thread, string, strips of printed papers such as wallpaper or sheets of magazines
3. ruler and pencil
4. scissors
5. paste or glue

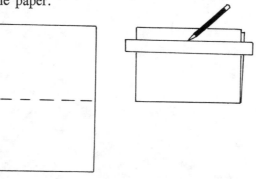

DISCOVERY STEPS:

1. Fold the paper in half, horizontally. Place paper on working surface, with open edges at the top. Draw a pencil line one inch down from the open edges, across the width of the paper.

2. Cut the weft strips, beginning at the fold and cutting to the pencil line. These may be curved, straight, zig-zag or any other irregular shape.

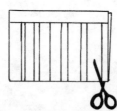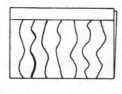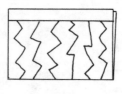

3. Weave in weft consisting of all the bits and pieces, using any of the patterns on pages 9–12.

4. When the weaving is completed, glue or paste down all the ends of the weft strips and trim edges.

weaving on cardboard

There are many advantages to this form of weaving. Cardboard is economical, easily obtained, and can be cut into various shapes and sizes. The warp and weft are easily arranged as the designer experiments. The cardboard may remain as background for the completed weaving, or the weaving may be removed from the cardboard and displayed as a woven form. The cardboard technique opens exciting new avenues for discovery.

MATERIALS:

for loom:

—stiff carton type of cardboard with the corrugations covered on both sides so the outside surfaces are smooth
—chipboard, medium and heavy weights
—shoe box lids or sturdy gift boxes
—illustration board
—cardboard containers such as those used for salt, oats, cottage cheese or sour cream

to cut: serrated knift, scissors, paper cutter and/or mat knife

warp strings:

cotton string, kite string, carpet warp, heavy yarn; anything without much elasticity.

weft threads:

roving (cotton)	wool yarns	weeds
twine	string	felt
lace	jute	velvet
rickrack	raffia	pipe cleaners
strips of cloth	ribbon	leather strips

other tools:

shuttle   beater   scissors   pencil and ruler

PREPARING THE CARDBOARD:

1. When using a cardboard box, cut into pieces using a serrated knife. Cut along the corner edges and the fold lines of the flaps.

2. For straight edges, cut the pieces into desired sizes on the paper cutter.

3. Suggested sizes:

   —for placemat: 12″ x 18″   —pocket or purse: 9″ x 12″
   —shapes: 12″ x 12″

a rectangular mat

Technique: cardboard

MATERIALS:

1. (1) 9″ x 12″ or 12″ x 18″ piece of cardboard
2. pencil and ruler
3. scissors
4. weft strings
5. warp threads
6. beater and shuttle

DISCOVERY STEPS:

THE LOOM:

1. Draw a pencil line ½″ to 1″ from the edge, both at the top and the bottom of the cardboard. This can be done vertically or horizontally. Make pencil marks at ½″ intervals along both pencil lines, beginning ¾″ to 1″ from the side edge and ending the same distance from the opposite side edge.

vertical:

horizontal:

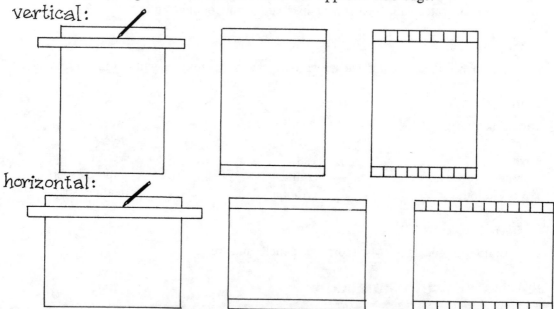

2. Using scissors, cut slits or "wedges" from the top and bottom edges to the points along the pencil lines as illustrated.

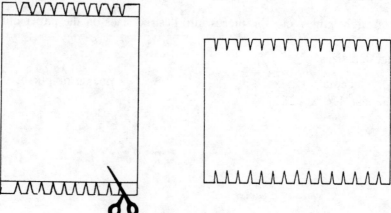

THE WARP:

1. Secure one end of the warp string, using either of the following methods:

   —tie one end of the warp around the first tab and secure with a knot.

   —put a knot in one end of the warp string and slip the knot between the first notch on the left.

2. Bring the warp string down the face of the loom to the first notch on the bottom edge, pulling it through to the back of the loom.

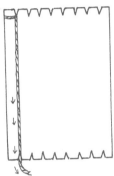

3. Loop warp around the back of the tab, through to the front of the second notch.

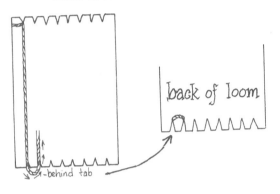

back of loom

-behind tab

4. Bring the warp back across the front of the loom to the second notch at the top and through to the back.

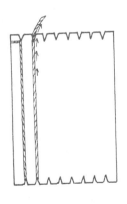

5. Loop warp around the back of the tab, to the front of the loom.

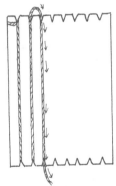

(The only warp string that will show on the back of the loom will be be small stitch-like threads between the notches.)

back of loom

6. Continue leading the warp back and forth across the face of the loom keeping the warp in parallel rows, pulling just tight enough so that it will lie flat on the cardboard. Tie off by securing in place around the last tab with a knot.

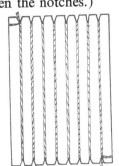

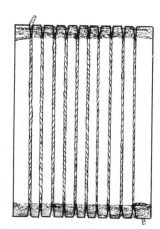

7. To insure that the tabs are not broken off during the weaving process, it is a good idea to bind the notched areas with masking tape, going over both rows of tabs, front and back, with a strip of masking tape (see shaded area of illustration).

THE WEFT:

weaver's knot

1. Begin by attaching the end of the first piece of weft thread to be used to the first right-hand warp thread using a *weaver's knot,* as illustrated.

2. Using a shuttle, pass the weft back and forth across the width of the loom. Don't be limited to row after row of tabby weave. Experiment with color, texture and a variety of weaving patterns (refer to pages 9–12).

3. Try combining tissue paper, reeds, cords, wool and string. Use strips of synthetic leathers, ribbon, lace, rickrack and any other found "bits and pieces."

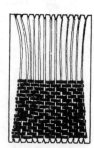

4. As the weft is pulled through for each row be sure that the outside edges are kept in a straight line. There is a tendency to pull the weft progressively tighter so that the edges curve inward. Don't leave it dangling in loops either as this will give the work a sloppy look.

A SPECIAL HINT:

As the illustration as the right shows, there is a tendency to pull the weft progressively tighter so that the edges curve. To eliminate this problem a row of stitches along each side of the loom can be made which will hold the weft threads in place and keep the edges straight. The following steps will show how to do this.

—With a pencil, make a series of dots ½″ to 1″ apart along each side of the loom. Punch a hole at each dot with a nail or embroidery needle.

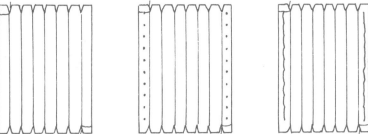

—Using an embroidery needle threaded with string, make a row of back stitches on each side as illustrated.

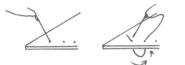   

—When weaving, the weft will be slipped under and over these stitches to hold the weft and keep the edges straight. When the weaving is completed, snip the stitches to release the weaving.

MATERIALS:

1. a rectangular piece of cardboard, any size desired.
2. ruler and pencil
3. scissors
4. warp string
5. weft threads
6. shuttle and beater
7. a large-eyed needle

a pocket or purse

DISCOVERY STEPS:

THE LOOM:

1. Measure, mark and cut the slits or "wedges" as for a rectangular mat (refer to pages 30–33). For a tighter weave, make the notches closer together. Use the cardboard vertically or horizontally.

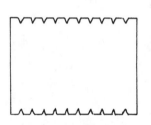

THE WARP:

To create the "pocket," the warp string will be on *both sides* of the loom.

1. Tie one end of the warp string around the first tab and secure with a knot.

2. Bring the warp string down the face of the loom to the first notch on the bottom edge; pull through to the back of the loom.

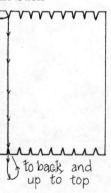

to back and up to top

3. Pull warp up the back of the loom, returning to the first top notch.

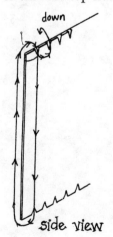

down

side view

4. After pulling warp through first notch back to the front of the loom, pull across to the right through the second notch to the back of the loom.

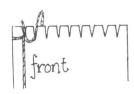

front

5. Bring the warp down the back of the loom to the bottom second notch, through to the front of the loom.

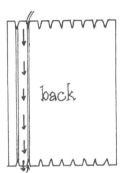

back

6. Bring the warp up the front of the loom, returning to second notch. Pull warp through to back, across to right in back through third notch to front of loom.

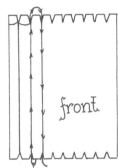

front

7. Continue in the same manner—keeping warp in parallel rows, pulling just tight enough so it will lie flat on the cardboard—ending at the top of the loom.

The arrows in the illustration show direction of warp.

REMEMBER: WARP WILL GO THROUGH BOTTOM NOTCHES ONCE AND EACH TOP NOTCH TWICE.

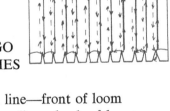

top

solid line—front of loom
broken line—back of loom

8. When warp is complete, secure tabs with masking tape so they won't break off during the weaving process.

THE WEFT:

1. Begin at the bottom of the loom (where warp goes through notches only once). Attach the end of the first piece of weft thread to the first right-hand warp thread, using a weaver's knot.

2. Weave the weft across the front of the loom, around the side and then across the back of the loom, weaving around and around the loom in a relatively tight pattern.

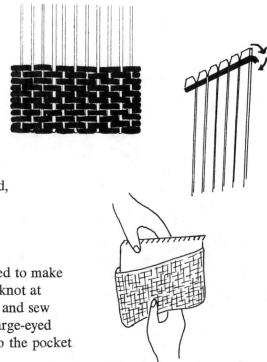

Push the weft down while weaving so it will be tight with no warp showing.

3. When the weaving is completed, bend the tabs at the top and slip the cardboard out of the weaving.

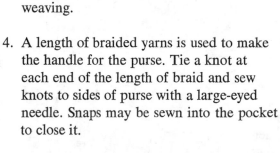

4. A length of braided yarns is used to make the handle for the purse. Tie a knot at each end of the length of braid and sew knots to sides of purse with a large-eyed needle. Snaps may be sewn into the pocket to close it.

5. Both the pocket and the purse can be lined with fabric if desired.

Technique: cardboard

anything goes

MATERIALS:

1. cardboard square or rectangle, any size desired
2. ruler and pencil
3. scissors
4. warp string
5. weft threads
6. shuttle and beater
7. large-eyed needle
8. "bits and pieces"

DISCOVERY STEPS:

1. Vary the warp string to create many interesting effects. Using the pencil and ruler, mark dots ½″ in from the edge of the cardboard, equally or unequally spaced across the top and bottom of all four edges. Cut slits or notches at each dot marked. The following are a few suggestions:

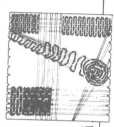

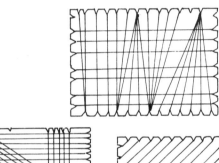

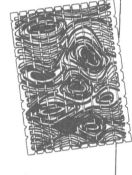

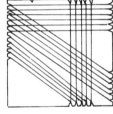

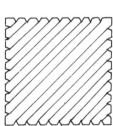

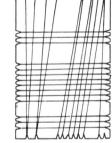

2. String the warp on one side of the loom (refer to pages 30–32). If desired, the cardboard may be painted or covered with plain or printed papers before stringing the warp. This will provide an interesting background if large open spaces are planned in the weaving.

3. Weaving the weft threads will be determined by the patterns created with the warp strings. Try weaving areas, long strips, overlapping and so forth. Incorporate other materials such as feathers, seashells, bits of ribbon, fabric, strips of paper and so forth.

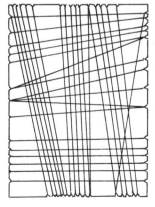

4. When the weaving is completed it can be left on the cardboard loom or removed by bending back the tabs and slipping off. To support and/or hang, slide sticks, dowels or twigs through the loops which were on the tabs.

a round mat

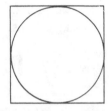

Technique: cardboard

MATERIALS:

1. square of cardboard, 9″ or 12″
2. compass
3. pencil and ruler
4. scissors
5. warp string
6. weft threads
7. shuttle and beater

DISCOVERY STEPS:

1. Using the compass, make
   a circle on the square
   of cardboard as large as
   the size permits. Trim
   away excess cardboard
   with scissors.

2. Using the compass and/or ruler, mark an *uneven number* of dots, ½″ from the
   edge, equally spaced. At each dot make a slit or wedge with the scissors.

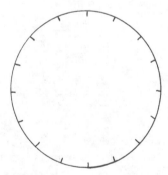

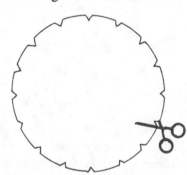

3. *To warp:*

   —Tie a knot at one end of
   the warp string. Slip the
   knot through one of the
   notches to anchor into
   place.

   —Pull the warp string across the
   face of the circle to the notch
   opposite; slip through notch,
   around the tab and up through
   the notch right next to it and
   to the front of the loom.

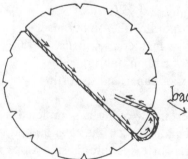

back of loom

—Pull the warp back across the face of the loom to the notch opposite, and next to the first notch. Continue in the same manner, back and forth across the face of the loom, pulling the warp just tight enough so that it will lie flat on the cardboard. Tie off with a knot.

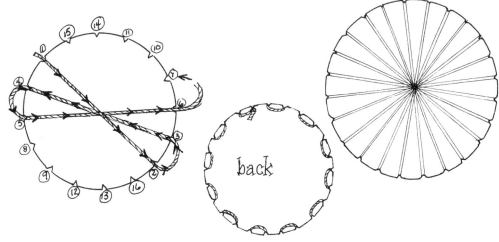

4. *The weft:*

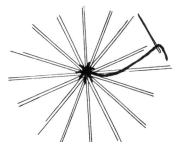

   —Begin by using a large-eyed needle, securing all the threads in the middle where they cross; pull the thread over and under all the threads making an "X" shape.

   —Weave, starting at the center, pulling the yarn snug to the center of the loom. If the circle is to be used as a hot pad, use the tabby weave so it will be tight and firm when completed.

   —When the weaving is finished, bend back the tabs to remove the weaving from the cardboard loom.

VARIATIONS:

—The following are a few examples of other ways to vary the warp:

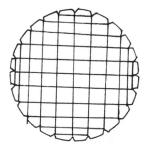 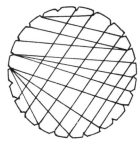 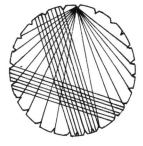

—Try warping both sides of the loom; weave and use as hanging ornamental discs.

Technique: cardboard

MATERIALS:

1. cardboard, size determined by shape
2. ½″ or ¼″ graph paper
3. pencil and ruler
4. newspaper
5. scissors
6. warp string
7. weft threads
8. shuttle and beater
9. "bits and pieces"

DISCOVERY STEPS:

1. Select a simple symmetrical shape. Experiment with folded newspaper; cut out a number of shapes and choose one.

  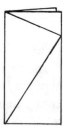

2. Place the selected shape on a piece of graph paper and trace around it. The graph paper aids in planning the direction the warp string will be placed. Cut out the shape. Using the markings on the graph paper, plan and mark where the notches will be made to anchor the warp string.

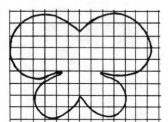 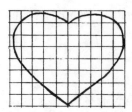 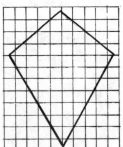

3. Place the graph paper shape on the cardboard and trace around it, marking the points where the notches will be made. Cut out shape and notches.

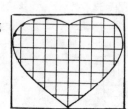 

4. Warp the loom on one side (refer to pages 30–32). The following illustrations will show how several shapes are warped.

 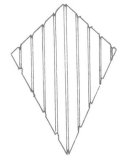 

5. *The weft:* use all kinds of yarns and other materials, experimenting with various weaving patterns.

6. When the weaving is completed, it can be left on the cardboard loom or taken off by bending the tabs down so that it will slip off easily.

on a shoe box lid

Technique: cardboard

MATERIALS:

1. shoe box lid or other shallow cardboard box
2. scissors and/or paper punch
3. pencil and ruler
4. warp string
5. weft thread
6. shuttle and beater
7. "bits and pieces"
*8. optional: tempera paint and paint brush or paper and glue or paste to decorate box

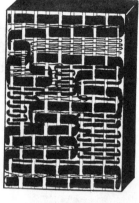

DISCOVERY STEPS:

1. Using the ruler and pencil, make an equal number of dots along two opposite edges of the box.

2. To hold the warp string, make notches at the dots on the opposite edges or use a paper punch and make holes.

*3. Attach one end of the warp string to the box with a knot or tie one end of the warp around the first tab and secure with a knot.

4. Pull the warp across the loom to the notch opposite, pull through the notch (or hole), loop around tab and through the second notch.

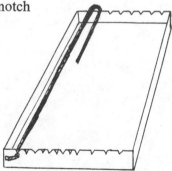

* If desired, the box may be painted with tempera paint or decorated with plain or printed paper before attaching the warp string and weft threads.

5. Pull the warp back across the loom to the opposite notch, pull through and loop around the back of the tab to the notch right next to it. Continue in the same manner, back and forth across the face of the loom until complete. Tie off warp string with a knot.

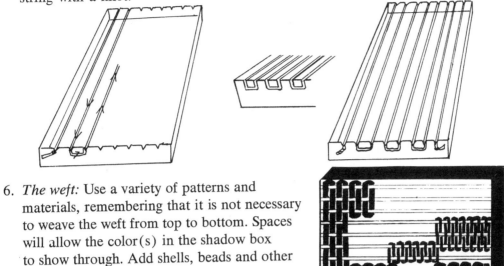

6. *The weft:* Use a variety of patterns and materials, remembering that it is not necessary to weave the weft from top to bottom. Spaces will allow the color(s) in the shadow box to show through. Add shells, beads and other "bits and pieces" to take advantage of the three-dimensional effect.

7. To remove, if desired, bend down the tabs and slip carefully off. Slide sticks or twigs through the loops to display or hang.

VARIATIONS:

—Try warping the loom in an irregular manner, using all four sides of the box. The following are a few examples. Also refer to page 37, "Anything Goes," for other ideas.

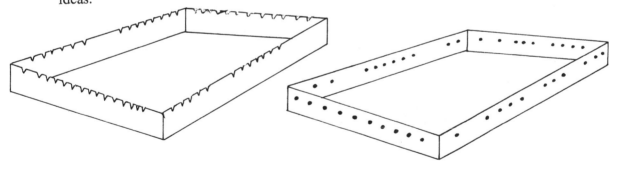

Technique: cardboard

MATERIALS:

1. a cardboard container such as one used for salt, oats, cottage cheese or sour cream
2. pencil and ruler
3. scissors
4. warp string
5. weft thread
6. tapestry needle (any needle with a large eye)
7. beater

DISCOVERY STEPS:

1. Around the bottom edge of the carton, put an unequal number of dots approximately ½″ apart. From the dots draw lines up the sides of the carton to the top.

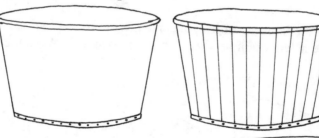

2. Using scissors, cut slits or wedges from the top edge of the carton at each line about ¼″ down. Clip the bottom edge of the carton at each dot, barely through the edge.

3. *The warp:*

   —Tie a knot at one end of the warp string. Insert the knot in a notch at the top of the carton, on the inside.

   —Pull the warp string down the side of the carton to the notch directly below on the bottom.

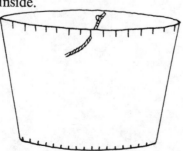

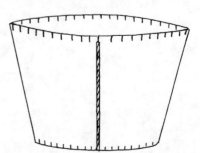

44

—Carry the warp string straight across the bottom into the opposite notch.

—Pull warp string up the side to notch right above on top, through notch, around tab and bring through notch directly to right.

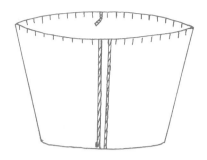

—Pull warp string down to bottom notch, across bottom to opposite edge and so on . . . continuing in the same manner, pulling the warp just tight enough so that it lies flat against the container. The warp threads on the bottom will be like the spokes of a wheel.

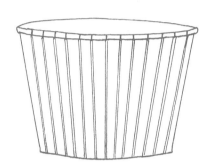

4. *The weft:*

—Start in the center, at the bottom, weaving over and under, pulling very tight at first to secure the center where all the strings cross. Weave loosely as the weft moves farther from the center.

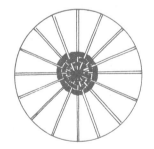

—When weaving around the sides of the carton push the weft down tightly with the beater.

—Use ribbon, wools and yarns of varying thickness for interest and texture.

—To remove carton, if desired, bend down tabs and carefully remove the carton off bottom of weaving. (It becomes a sort of "pocket" weaving.)

VARIATIONS:

—The "shoulder bag" was made on an oats container and is perfect for a knitting bag.

—It is also possible to use square containers such as those used to hold washing soap, etc.

weaving into scrim

Imaginative patterns can be made by weaving colorful threads into the fabric background of scrim, sometimes called cross-stitch rug canvas. The fairly large holes in the construction permit thread and yarn to be easily pushed or pulled through the mesh.

MATERIALS:

1. piece of scrim, any size desired
2. scissors
3. weft threads: yarn, string, roving, embroidery threads, "bits and pieces"
4. glue or paste
5. large-eyed needle
6. optional: plain newsprint, crayons and/or felt tip pen

DISCOVERY STEPS:

1. Cut scrim to desired size.

2. The weaving may be done spontaneously into the scrim material or pre-planned and transferred to the scrim in the following manner:

   —Draw a design on a piece of newsprint the same size as the scrim, keeping the shapes or design fairly large and simple.

—Place the scrim on top of the paper with the design. It will show through the scrim.

—Use a crayon or felt tip pen to trace over the design, putting the lines on the scrim.

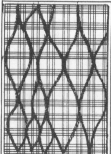 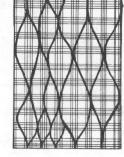

3. Weave over-and-under the scrim fibers to outline the shape or, with same weaving procedure, fill in solid areas. The illustration shows weaving in scrim with a large-eyed needle.

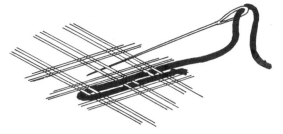

4. Although the basic weave is over-and-under, the following will illustrate a few of the many possibilities:

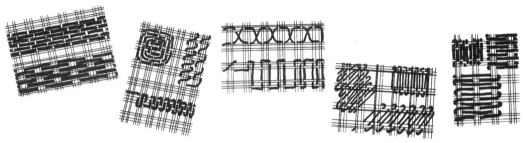

VARIATIONS:

—Cut out areas and make the yarns or threads span the open spaces, or hang things such as bells in the spaces.

—Cut shapes out of scrim, weave and hang as parts of of a mobile or individually.

weaving into cotton mesh

Many types of cotton mesh provide weaving possibilities. The mesh serves as a background, with threads woven into the material to form patterns. Cotton mesh is available in curtains, mosquito netting, onion bags and dish cloths. It may also be purchased by the yard or collected from scraps.

MATERIALS:

1. cotton mesh netting, size desired
2. old picture frame or wood frame
3. stapler
4. weft threads: yarns, embroidery threads, "bits and pieces"
5. large-eyed needle
6. scissors

DISCOVERY STEPS:

1. Mesh is a flimsy material and works best when fastened to a frame.

   —wood frame: refer to page 52 for directions on how to make a simple wood frame, or use an old picture frame.
   —cardboard frame: staple or glue 1½" wide strips of cardboard together to make a frame to staple the mesh to.

2. Stretching the mesh:

   Cut a piece of mesh a little bit larger than the frame to be used. Place the mesh on top of the frame. Staple mesh to frame along one edge. Pull mesh from opposite edge until it is taut and then staple to opposite edge. Finally, staple sides.

3. *THE WEFT:*
   —Work spontaneously, weaving directly into the mesh without previous planning, or use the procedure followed in weaving scrim, drawing design first on paper and then transferring to the cotton mesh.
   —With a needle and thread, outline and fill in the design. Make some lines straight, some wavy or circular.
   —Experiment with unusual material, weaving such things as dried grasses, dried flowers, and other "bits and pieces" into the mesh.

VARIATIONS:

—Completed weavings may be stitched together to make a wall hanging or displayed individually on dowel or wire rods.

48

—Use a large-eyed needle to weave.

—Try the following:

under-one-over-one

over-three-under-one

—Use any of the traditional weaving patterns using one or more weft strings.

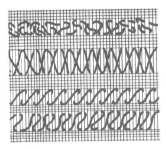

under-two-
over-two

under-three
- over-three

—Weave in an irregular pattern such as:

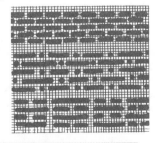

—Move some of the remaining weft threads up or down to form curved lines.

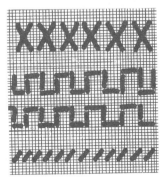

—Tie groups of warp threads together to create spaces, equally or unequally spaced.

4. When the weaving is completed, fold over the top about 1½″ and sew or glue to a dowel rod for hanging. Fringe about 2″ at the bottom. The fringe threads may be tied together in groups or left as is.

VARIATIONS:

As burlap is very loosely woven it lends itself to other weaving projects. By weaving different sets or combinations, such as over-two-under-two, interesting patterns will develop. These can be done on small squares, on a wall hanging, or included in the drawn thread project above.

MATERIALS:

* 1. two 1″ x 1″ pieces of soft pine, of equal length, for top and bottom of loom
2. two 1″ x 1″ pieces of soft pine, equal length but longer, for sides of loom
3. 1″ nails and hammer
4. ruler and pencil
5. warp string
6. weft threads
7. "bits and pieces"
8. scissors, shuttle and beater

a wooden loom

DISCOVERY STEPS:

* 1. When making the wooden loom for the first time the following sizes are suggested:

    short pieces: 9″   long pieces: 12″
or short pieces: 12″ long pieces: 18″

2. To make the wooden loom place the two longer pieces of wood on a flat surface, parallel to each other. Place the two shorter pieces, one at each end, on top (as illustrated), and nail into place. Make sure ends are even. Use two nails at each corner to secure.

3. Using the ruler and pencil, measure and mark dots every half-inch down the center of the top surface of the short strips of wood. Following this, drive a 1″ nail at each dot, half-way down the wood, and slant them toward the outside. If desired, "staple" nails may be used instead of nails; this will add more strings to the warp.

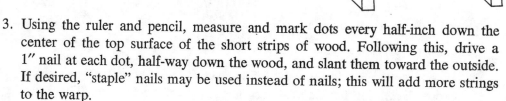

4. To warp: Start at any corner and tie one end of the warp string to the corner nail. Pull the warp string across the face of the loom to the nail opposite. Wrap the warp string around the back of the first two nails as illustrated:

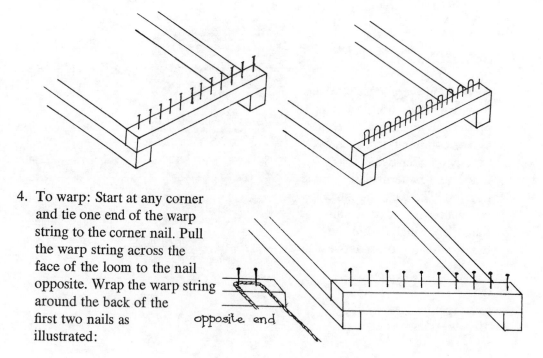

opposite end

52

5. Pull the warp string back across the face of the loom to the nails opposite. Wrap around nails two and three. Continue in the same manner, back and forth across the face of the loom. This will put the warp strings parallel at half-inch intervals, making it easier to use. If a tighter weave is desired, the nails can be placed closer together. Pull the warp string just tight enough so that the strings don't sag and it will be easy to weave through.

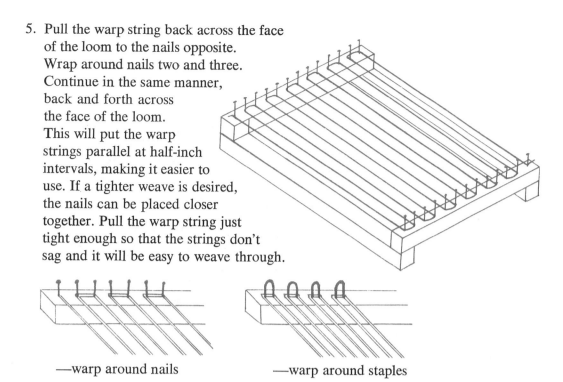

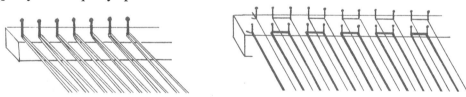

—warp around nails   —warp around staples

6. The weft: Using the shuttle and beater, weave any patterns desired. Experiment! Don't be limited to wool yarns and threads. Weave with all kinds of paper, strips of fabric, ribbons, twine, weeds and other "bits and pieces." Refer to the tapestry techniques on pages 10–12 for other ideas.

7. To remove weaving, refer to page 17.

VARIATIONS:

—To vary the warp, and create more strings, arrange the nails in patterns, either equally or unequally spaced:

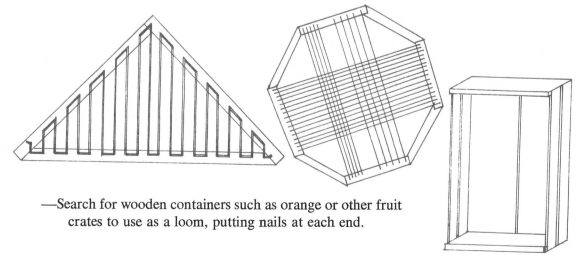

—Make a frame in separate sections fitted together for large unusual shapes:

—Search for wooden containers such as orange or other fruit crates to use as a loom, putting nails at each end.

a table mat

Technique: wooden loom

MATERIALS:

1. 4 pieces of wood, 1″ by 7⅜″
2. 1″ nails
3. hammer
4. ruler and pencil
5. warp strings
6. weft threads: yarn, wool or synthetic
7. scissors
8. large-eyed needle

DISCOVERY STEPS:

1. Put strips of wood together as illustrated to make the loom:

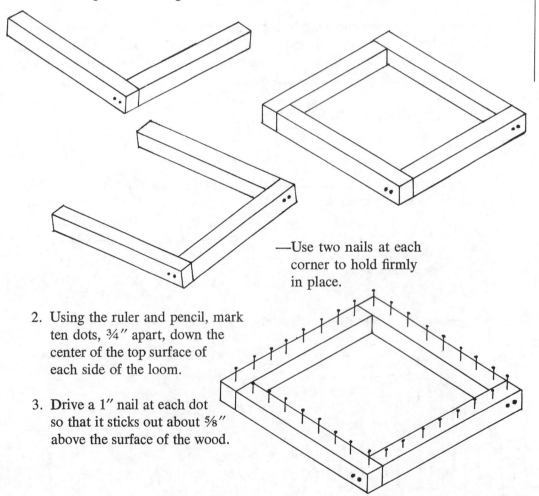

—Use two nails at each corner to hold firmly in place.

2. Using the ruler and pencil, mark ten dots, ¾″ apart, down the center of the top surface of each side of the loom.

3. Drive a 1″ nail at each dot so that it sticks out about ⅝″ above the surface of the wood.

4. Tie one end of wool yarn to one corner nail and wind as illustrated. The dark line is the first complete wind of the loom and the gray is the second winding of the loom. Repeat until there are about 8–10 thicknesses of yarn between the nails.

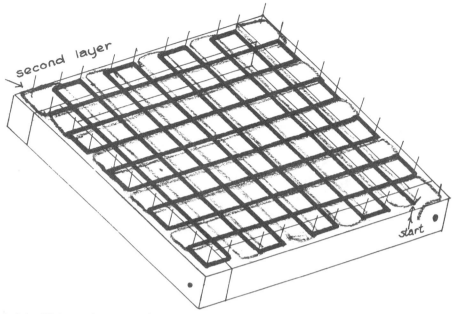

5. To finish: Using a large-eyed needle and pieces of yarn, make a knot around each point where the yarn crosses; contrasting colors will make it more interesting.

6. To remove the mat, ease it gently from the nails and tuck in any yarn ends. The loops along the edges can be cut for a tufted effect if desired.

VARIATIONS:

—Using a frame 12″ x 18″, make placemats. The yarn will only have to be wound to about 4–5 thicknesses.

Tapestry weaving employs the basic technique of linking areas of adjacent threads which may be similar or different in color. This is done by interlocking strands of single, double or even triple threads.

MATERIALS:

1. cardboard or wooden loom
2. warp strings
3. weft threads
4. "bits and pieces"
5. scissors, large-eyed needle
6. shuttle and beater
8. materials to hang: refer to page 17.

DISCOVERY STEPS:

1. Prepare the loom, cardboard or wooden. It can be any size desired.

2. String the warp.

3. The weaving can be done spontaneously or pre-planned. To plan, draw the shape or design on paper, using crayon to plan the areas of color. Large areas of color work best. After the warp is stretched, the prepared design can be slipped under the strands of warp as a guide.

4. To hang the completed weaving, refer to page 51.

HINTS:

—It is easier to weave the shape first and then the background.
—Be sure to plan the tapestry slits so they don't appear to be just a series of holes.
—The following illustrations are reminders; refer to pages 10–12.

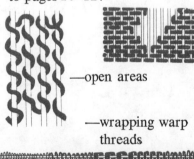
—open areas
—wrapping warp threads

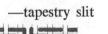
—tapestry slit

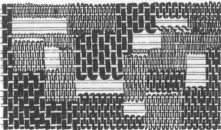

—interlocking threads

—eccentric weft
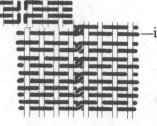

56

spool weaving

MATERIALS:

- —(1) large wooden thread spool
- —(4–8) 1″ finishing nails
- —yarn
- —crochet hook, small
- —optional: large-eyed needles, bells, wooden beads for belt
- —hammer

DISCOVERY STEPS:

1. Hammer the finishing nails in one end of the wooden spool as illustrated, making sure they are evenly spaced. Let the nails extend out from the top about ½″.
For easier weaving, two nails instead of one or staples may be used. This will make it easier to pick up the loops when weaving.

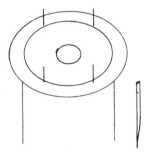  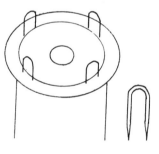

2. to warp:

—Drop one end of the yarn through the hole in the spool and let the end stick out of the hole at the bottom.

—Loop the yarn once around each nail or pair of nails COUNTER-CLOCKWISE, as shown:

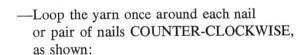

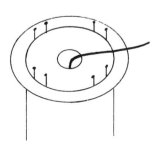 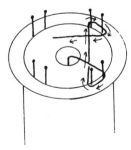 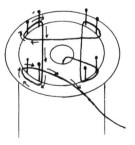

3. After winding the yarn around the nails counter-clockwise once, bring the yarn around the front of nails, above loops; hold with the left hand.

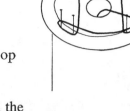

Using the crochet hook, pick up the bottom loop of the first pair of nails, lift over yarn and top of nails, dropping loop into the center. Continue around each set of nails and then pull the tail at the bottom of the spool to pull loops into position.

4. Continue, following the same steps in #3, wrapping the yarn around the outside of the nails, bringing the bottom loop up over the top yarn and nails, dropping loop into the center.

5. To cast off, take the last loop made off the nails and place it over the nails to the left; pick up the bottom loop, slip it over the top loop and nails to the center. Continue placing the remaining loops over the nails to the left until only one loop remains. Cut the yarn about 3″ above the last loop and pull end of yarn through the final loop.

6. The long strands of weaving can be made into a belt, sewn together to make mats or pads as well as wide belts and so forth.

ojo de dios

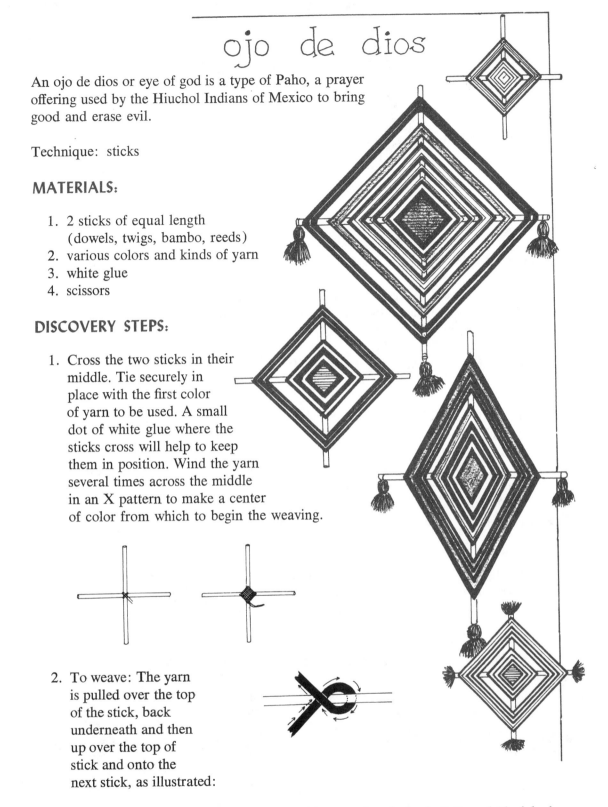

An ojo de dios or eye of god is a type of Paho, a prayer offering used by the Hiuchol Indians of Mexico to bring good and erase evil.

Technique: sticks

MATERIALS:

1. 2 sticks of equal length (dowels, twigs, bambo, reeds)
2. various colors and kinds of yarn
3. white glue
4. scissors

DISCOVERY STEPS:

1. Cross the two sticks in their middle. Tie securely in place with the first color of yarn to be used. A small dot of white glue where the sticks cross will help to keep them in position. Wind the yarn several times across the middle in an X pattern to make a center of color from which to begin the weaving.

2. To weave: The yarn is pulled over the top of the stick, back underneath and then up over the top of stick and onto the next stick, as illustrated:

3. Think of the sticks as being in these positions on the clock: 3, 6, 9, and 12 o'clock. Work COUNTER-CLOCKWISE, pulling the yarn just tight enough so that it lies flat and does not sag between the sticks.

—Pull the yarn over the top of the 3 o'clock stick, back underneath itself and then over the top on to the 12 o'clock stick.

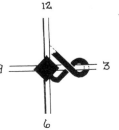

—Pull the yarn over the top of the 12 o'clock stick, back underneath itself and then up over the top on to the 9 o'clock stick.

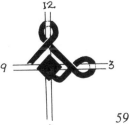

59

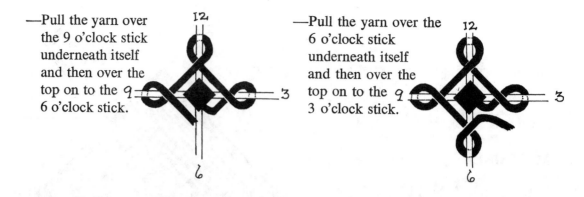

—Pull the yarn over the 9 o'clock stick underneath itself and then over the top on to the 6 o'clock stick.

—Pull the yarn over the 6 o'clock stick underneath itself and then over the top on to the 3 o'clock stick.

4. Continue in the same manner, making sure that each time the yarn is wrapped around the stick it lies flat and right next to, not overlapping, the yarn already there.

   If spaces are desired between colors, wrap the yarn around the stick an equal number of times on each stick before going on to the next stick, or use the technique described below.

   To change colors of yarn, knot a new color to the end of the yarn used, trim ends and continue.

5. The design should be finished with about 1″ of stick end exposed. The stick ends can be left plain or wrapped with yarn and secured with glue.

6. Add a tassel to the end of each stick. Refer to page 12 for directions on making tassels.

VARIATIONS:

—To create a three-dimensional effect, reverse the weaving pattern; pull the yarn under the stick, over the top of the stick, back underneath and on to the next stick, working counter-clockwise or clockwise.

The following illustrates one complete round of the sticks reversing the pattern:

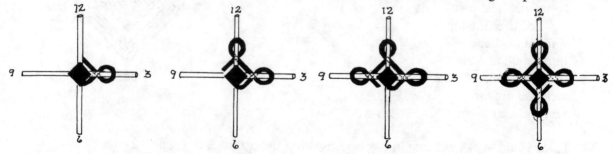

By alternating the weaving patterns, very interesting effects can be created.

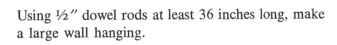

Using ½″ dowel rods at least 36 inches long, make a large wall hanging.

Begin by making one large god's eye in the center. Make additional ones by adding small sticks at the end of each main stick.

A whole wall piece can be made by continuing in the same manner, connecting many together.

A group of ojo de dios may be grouped together vertically or horizontally to make a design.

Using toothpicks, lollipop sticks, bamboo sticks or wire from coat hangers, make god's eyes of all sizes.

Use to make a mobile or hang individually as ornaments for a Christmas tree.

Combine several different sizes to suspend as a mobile.

Hang individually as ornaments on a Christmas tree. With the addition of metallic threads, they will glitter and shine on tree.

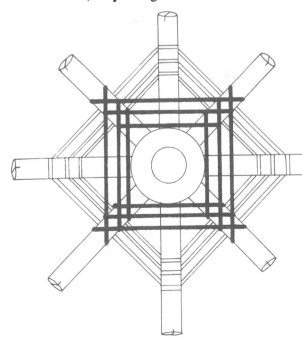

Experiment with wooden spool and dowel construction toys. Put a drop of glue on the tips of four or eight dowels and insert them in a spool. Weave like the ojo de dios, using both weaving patterns to create a three-dimensional effect.

MATERIALS:

with drinking straws

1. drinking straws
2. warp strings
3. weft threads: yarns of all kinds
4. scissors
5. shuttle and beater

DISCOVERY STEPS:

1. Cut the warp strings as long as the finished product is to be, i.e., belt—30″. Use an uneven number: 5, 7, 9, depending on the width desired. All warp strings should be the same length.

2. Cut the drinking straws in half, one half for each warp string.

3. Tie all the warp strings together at one end in a knot.

4. Thread the other ends of the warp strings through the straws as illustrated. Push the straws up to the knotted ends.

5. For easier weaving, secure the knot in a clipboard or use a hook made of wire or a piece of string to tie the knot to the back of a chair, door handle, etc., so the weaving can progress without having to struggle with holding the straws as well as weaving the weft.

6. Tie one end of the weft thread to one outside warp string next to the knot. Weave under and over the straws. As the weaving progresses, push the woven section up and off the straws, freeing them for more weaving. Add a new color by tying a knot to the previous color and continue the weaving.

7. Slip the straws off the warp when the weaving is completed and tie the warp strings together with a knot.

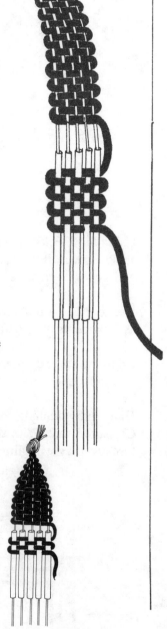

VARIATIONS:

—Use several strands of warp through each straw. This will provide more warp threads and make it possible to weave more intricate patterns.

—Sew completed pieces into new forms such as handbags.

62

on a coat hanger

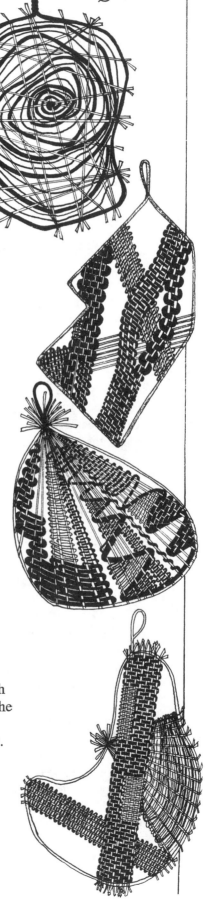

MATERIALS:

1. wire coat hanger
2. warp strings
3. weft threads
4. "bits and pieces"
5. scissors
6. large-eyed needle
7. shuttle and beater

DISCOVERY STEPS:

1. Holding the top of the hanger with one hand, pull the bottom and sides of the hanger with the other hand to stretch and bend into an interesting shape.

2. The hook at the top can be bent to close into a loop and wrapped with yarn or string.

3. The wire loom can be left as is or the wire can be covered by wrapping with yarn, string, strips of fabric or anything else, using a little glue to secure in place. This will help when warping because it will keep the warp strings from sliding on the smooth wire.

4. The warp: As the wire is smooth, the warp strings will slip unless secured into place either with glue or tied with small pieces of yarn or string. If the wire has been wrapped this will not be necessary. String the warp in any regular or irregular manner.

5. The weft: Weaving the weft threads will be determined by the patterns created by the warp threads. Try weaving areas, long strips, over-lapping and so forth. Incorporate "bits and pieces" and other found objects for interest.

63

MATERIALS:

1. branches (see #1 below)
2. warp strings
3. weft threads
4. "bits and pieces"
5. scissors
6. white glue
7. serrated knife
8. shuttle and beater
9. large-eyed needle

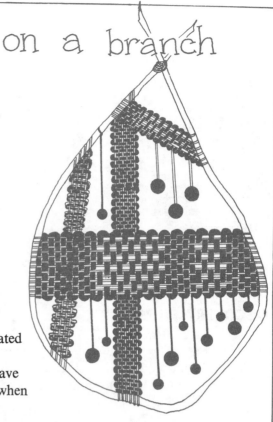

on a branch

DISCOVERY STEPS:

1. Use branches from deciduous trees. Prune away those twigs and side branches which will not be incorporated in the weaving. Use green branches. They're easier to use because they have less tendency to split than dry ones when bent into shapes.

2. Whole branches can be gently bent into circular or oval shapes. Lash the ends together with string or strips of leather. Cross the string over and around the branch ends where they overlap several times until they feel secure. Tie the ends of the string in knots and trim the ends.

3. The warp strings can be strung in any direction desired. One problem to contend with when warping is the strings slipping on the rounded branches. To eliminate this, slits or notches can be made in the branch with the serrated knife, and the warp string inserted into the slit. A dot of white glue can be added to each slit for added security. The branch itself can be wrapped with string or yarns before warping, serving both as a decorative means and also to hold the warp strings in position.

4. When weaving, use all kinds of weft threads as well as "bits and pieces." Think about adding pieces of bark, weed stems, twigs, vines and seedpods which are effective additions to this kind of weaving. Bells, beads, and so forth, can also be incorporated.

64